Copyright © 1985 Uitgeversmij J.H. Kok BV, Kampen, The Netherlands

Published by
**Lion Publishing plc**
Sandy Lane West, Oxford, England
ISBN 0 7459 2213 9
**Albatross Books Pty Ltd**
PO Box 320, Sutherland, NSW 2232, Australia
ISBN 0 7324 0610 2

First edition 1986
Reprinted 1988
This edition 1992

A catalogue record for this book is available
from the British Library

Printed and bound by Mohndruck in Germany.
Origination: Fotolitho Boan BV, Utrecht

# The Ark

A LION BOOK
Oxford · Batavia · Sydney

When I feel a painting is finished, I put it
on one side for a time. In this way I can
keep an eye on it while working on
something else. I glance at it from
time to time — then sometimes, all at
once, I can see what may have been bothering me about it.

This painting, for
instance — the boars
crossing the ditch onto
the farmland.
There's nothing
unusual about this
— it's just how it
was...
But still, that big
empty space where
nothing at all was
happening was
frankly boring.

So I had another go.

This one started like this — I thought
it rather a nice painting.
"Roebuck on the Moor"
But when I had changed it, it
pleased me even more.
This way it showed much more clearly
how vast the world is to a
small roebuck.
And that was the point.

This sort of thing you sometimes only
notice afterwards.

It was in just this sort of way that
I could not work out for some time what these two
paintings kept reminding me of — great dark skies,
the water, one lonely bird — until suddenly I had it :
NOAH AND THE ARK !

Noah's Ark amongst
the flooded treetops
of Mount Ararat

# The Great Flood

Noah was a just man and perfect in his generations, and Noah walked with God. And Noah begat three sons, Shem, Ham, and Japheth. The earth also was corrupt before God, and the earth was filled with violence. And God looked upon the earth, and, behold, it was corrupt; for all flesh had corrupted his way upon the earth.

And God said unto Noah, The end of all flesh is come before me; for the earth is filled with violence through them; and, behold, I will destroy them with the earth. Make thee an ark of gopher wood; rooms shalt thou make in the ark, and shalt pitch it within and without with pitch. And this is the fashion which thou shalt make it of: The length of the ark shall be three hundred cubits, the breadth of it fifty cubits, and the height of it thirty cubits. A window shalt thou make to the ark, and in a cubit shalt thou finish it above; and the door of the ark shalt thou set in the side thereof; with lower, second, and third stories shalt thou make it. And, behold, I, even I, do bring a flood of waters upon the earth, to destroy all flesh, wherein is the breath of life, from under heaven; and every thing that is in the earth shall die. But with thee will I establish my covenant; and thou shalt come into the ark, thou, and thy sons, and thy wife, and thy sons' wives with thee. And of every living thing of all flesh, two of every sort shalt thou bring into the ark, to keep them alive with thee; they shall be male and female. Of fowls after their kind, and of cattle after their kind, of every creeping thing of the earth after his kind, two of every sort shall come unto thee, to keep them alive. And take thou unto thee of all food that is eaten, and thou shalt gather it to thee; and it shall be for food for thee, and for them. Thus did Noah; according to all that God commanded him, so did he.

And the Lord said unto Noah, Come thou and all thy house into the ark; for thee have I seen righteous before me in this generation. Of every clean beast thou shalt take to thee by sevens, the male and his female: and of beasts that are not clean by two, the male and his female. Of fowls also of the air by sevens, the male and the female; to keep seed alive upon the face of all the earth. For yet seven days, and I will cause it to rain upon the earth forty days and forty nights; and every living substance that I have made will I destroy from off the face of the earth. And Noah did according unto all that the Lord commanded him. And Noah was six hundred years old when the flood of waters was upon the earth.

And Noah went in, and his sons, and his wife, and his sons' wives with him, into the ark, because of the waters of the flood. Of clean beasts, and of beasts that are not clean, and of fowls, and of every thing that creepeth upon the earth, There went in two and two unto Noah into the ark, the male and the female, as God had commanded Noah. And it came to pass after seven days, that the waters of the flood were upon the earth.

In the six hundredth year of Noah's life, in the second month, the seventeenth day of the month, the same day were all the fountains of the great deep broken up, and the windows of heaven were opened. And the rain was upon the earth forty days and forty nights. In the selfsame day entered Noah, and Shem, and Ham, and Japheth, the sons of Noah, and Noah's wife, and the three wives of his sons with them, into the ark; They, and every beast after his kind, and all the cattle after their kind, and every creeping thing that creepeth upon the earth after his kind, and every fowl after his kind, every bird of every sort. And they went in unto Noah into the ark, two and two of all flesh, wherein is the breath of life. And they that went in, went in male and female of all flesh, as God had commanded him: and the Lord shut him in. And the flood was forty days

upon the earth; and the waters increased, and bare up the ark, and it was lift up above the earth. And the waters prevailed, and were increased greatly upon the earth; and the ark went upon the face of the waters. And the waters prevailed exceedingly upon the earth; and all the high hills, that were under the whole heaven, were covered. Fifteen cubits upward did the waters prevail; and the mountains were covered. And all flesh died that moved upon the earth, both of fowl, and of cattle, and of beast, and of every creeping thing that creepeth upon the earth, and every man: All in whose nostrils was the breath of life, of all that was in the dry land, died. And every living substance was destroyed which was upon the face of the ground, both man, and cattle, and the creeping things, and the fowl of the heaven; and they were destroyed from the earth: and Noah only remained alive, and they that were with him in the ark. And the waters prevailed upon the earth an hundred and fifty days.

And God remembered Noah, and every living thing, and all the cattle that was with him in the ark: and God made a wind to pass over the earth, and the waters asswaged; The fountains also of the deep and the windows of heaven were stopped, and the rain from heaven was restrained; And the waters returned from off the earth continually: and after the end of the hundred and fifty days the waters were abated. And the ark rested in the seventh month, on the seventeenth day of the month, upon the mountains of Ararat. And the waters decreased continually until the tenth month: in the tenth month, on the first day of the month, were the tops of the mountains seen.

And it came to pass at the end of forty days, that Noah opened the window of the ark which he had made: And he sent forth a raven, which went forth to and fro, until the waters were dried up from off the earth. Also he sent forth a dove from him, to see if the waters were abated from off the face of the ground; But the dove found no rest for the sole of her foot, and she returned unto him into the ark, for the waters were on the face of the whole earth: then he put forth his hand, and took her, and pulled her in unto him into the ark. And he stayed yet other seven days; and again he sent forth the dove out of the ark; And the dove came in to him in the evening; and, lo, in her mouth was an olive leaf pluckt off: so Noah knew that the waters were abated from off the earth. And he stayed yet other seven days; and sent forth the dove; which returned not again unto him any more.

And it came to pass in the six hundredth and first year, in the first month, the first day of the month, the waters were dried up from off the earth: and Noah removed the covering of the ark, and looked, and, behold, the face of the ground was dry. And in the second month, on the seven and twentieth day of the month, was the earth dried.

And God spake unto Noah, saying, Go forth of the ark, thou, and thy wife, and thy sons, and thy sons' wives with thee. Bring forth with thee every living thing that is with thee, of all flesh, both of fowl, and of cattle, and of every creeping thing that creepeth upon the earth; that they may breed abundantly in the earth, and be fruitful, and multiply upon the earth. And Noah went forth, and his sons, and his wife, and his sons' wives with him: Every beast, every creeping thing, and every fowl, and whatsoever creepeth upon the earth, after their kinds, went forth out of the ark.

From Genesis, chapters 6-8

This is the story of Noah's Ark. You can read it in the first book of the Bible, Genesis. For those who have difficulty with this story (and the other ancient stories of the Bible like the Creation, the Garden of Eden, the Tower of Babel, and so on) here is another tale to keep next to it.

There was once a peasant who, every day at dusk, used to put a small dish of milk onto the low brick wall around his farmyard. Actually he could scarcely spare it, but this was his daily offering to God. In the morning the dish was always empty.

One day, just as the peasant is putting out the dish, along comes old Know-It-All and asks what all this is about. He is told that it is an offering to God which is accepted every night.

This seems too simple to Know-It-All.
"Oh, my good man, this is not quite what it seems...!
Tonight, by the light of the moon, we shall see what really happens." Seated side by side in a crooked shed, they peep out through the cracks at the dish on the wall.

And yes — within a couple of hours a scrubby fox suddenly sneaks up onto the wall, quickly laps up the milk and disappears.
"Now, what did I tell you?" Know-It-All smiles and triumphantly slaps the dazed peasant on the shoulder.
    "That's how it is!"

Then in a dream God appears to Know-It-All and says:
"Know-It-All, Know-It-All, what have you achieved by doing this? The peasant did a good deed for me. Personally I do not drink milk ... but I could be of some help to that poor miserable fox ..."

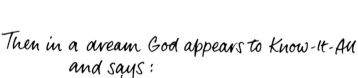

So, you see ...

A year or so ago in Holland there were a couple of special TV features on the Ark. You could see what the Ark must have looked like; actually more box than boat, the same uninteresting shape as the barns of present-day industrial farming.

Oddly enough...

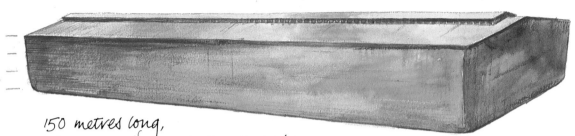

150 metres long, 25 metres wide and 15 metres high. It had three storeys. In a book on the Ark, Dr W.J. Ouweneel figured out that this was equivalent to 19,870 tons or, say, 750 truck loads.

"Make an ark of gopher wood," Noah was told. That's sooner said than done! I have just finished constructing one of the many little stalls I have in my yard, for the small goats.

And while sawing and hammering I have often thought of Noah — a lot of timber must have gone through his hands!

Many trees must have been felled. Maybe they were loaded the way it is still done in the Pijnenburger woods. Who knows, perhaps they used a timber wagon like this one.

The story of the Ark is often pictured in the period of the dinosaurs, but according to Dr Ouweneel the "assumption is justified that all this happened not more than ± 5,000 years ago, and certainly not more than ± 7,000 years ago." And by that time surely there were horses!

The lions that pursued the first Christians about 2,000 years ago and the ones that sat in the den with Daniel even earlier must have looked much the same as lions do today.

Noah

Shem

Ham

Japheth

In those days they had iron — an older brother of Noah, Tubal-cain, has been called "the father of blacksmiths"

It's possible they could have had a crane like this...

And even if the crane had not yet been invented, they still had horses

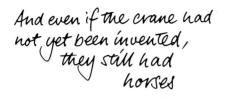

and with the help of elephants they could have moved mountains.

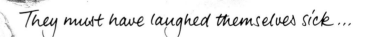

One thing is for sure: Noah must have attracted a great deal of attention. How people must have laughed ... What a duffer!

They must have laughed themselves sick ...

...But perhaps there were others ↗ who were not that stupid, who paid rather closer attention.

Perhaps they sensed that something
very special was going on

Animals are always on the
alert — and before people
have got wind of it they
sense an impending disaster.

Whether there was ridicule
or close attention
   Noah just went on
   with his carpentry
   ...year in, year out.

I asked a shipbuilder how he thought the Ark
would have been built.
"The same way other wooden boats are
built — but a great deal bigger."

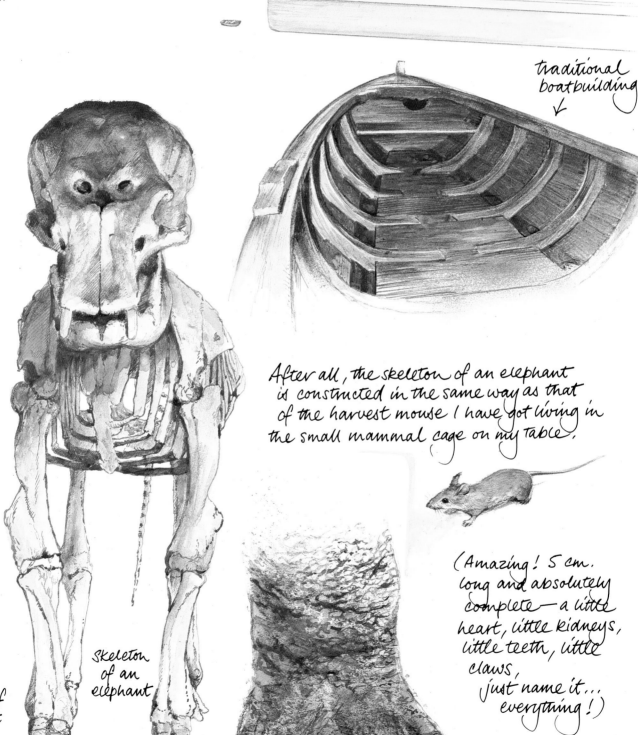

traditional
boatbuilding
↓

After all, the skeleton of an elephant
is constructed in the same way as that
of the harvest mouse I have got living in
the small mammal cage on my table.

(Amazing! 5 cm.
long and absolutely
complete — a little
heart, little kidneys,
little teeth, little
claws,
   just name it...
   everything!)

skeleton
of an
elephant

skeleton of
a harvest
mouse
↓

"... rooms shalt thou make in the Ark ..."
In the Great Bible of Mortier of 1702 you can find this delightful
illustration. Being an enthusiastic builder of small animal stalls I find
this a splendid picture!

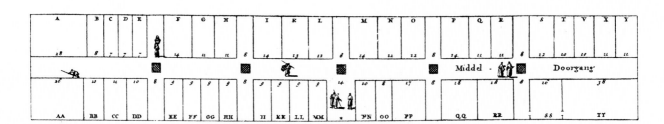

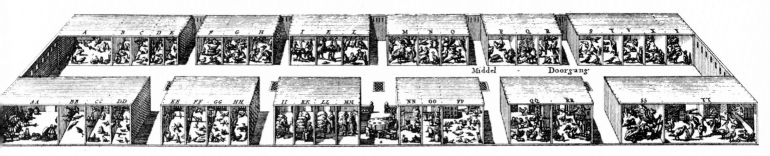

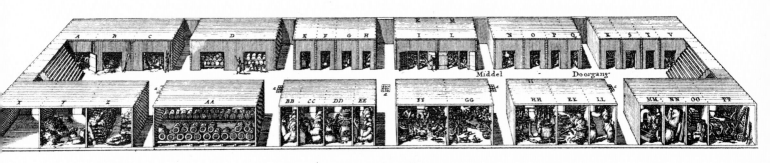

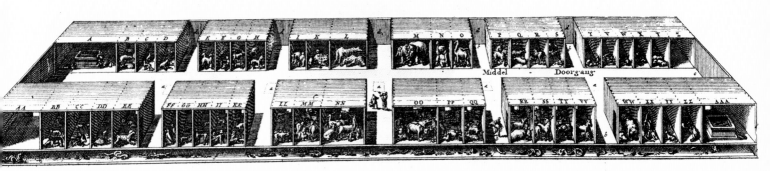

Upper, second and lowest
storeys of the Ark (Genesis 6)

Bovenste, tweede ende benedenste verdieping der Arke
Gen. VI

It could also be that different sizes of compartments were built, to allow more animals to be stowed aboard: spacious holds for the big animals, others for the medium-sized, smaller compartments for the smaller animals and, perhaps, a compartment for birds only, with perches.

5 metres

The three storeys of the Ark were each 5 metres high. That was really only necessary for the elephants and giraffes.

It would have been squandering space to give a pair of Patagonian hares a narrow stall 5 metres high — sheer waste.

The design of the compartments must have been something like this.

Noah himself would not have had a cabin 5 metres high, of course. He would have constructed a sleeping loft.

"...and the door of the ark shalt thou set in the side thereof..."

not in the lowest storey
it seems to me —

I have always thought of it
something like this

Swedish farmhouses
often have an entrance
built like this.

Once inside there are ramps
—one to the upper floor,
another to the lower floor.
(It's something like the flap
of a cattle truck, but a bit
stronger, because a fellow like
this may well weigh 2 tons)

and the white
rhinoceros easily
weighs three tons...

and of course this six-tonner had to get in too.

After all the carpenter's work had been done, the family started to tar the boat, inside and out — not a simple job at all ( I know all about that; during my time in the Navy I have been suspended alongside my ship like this, painting the topsides as punishment.)

And of course afterward they left the Ark for a while until the smell was gone.

You may well ask, wouldn't it have been much easier if God had just "created" an Ark himself ? Not if you think about it ! Clearly things do not work that way: whatever we can handle we apparently have to do ourselves.

straw for the animals quarters

When the job was nearly done, they must have peered at the skies now and then: how about those rains that were supposed to be coming ?

Seven days before the flood,
Noah got orders to go
aboard with his
family, and at the
same time the
miracle began:
the animals
started to
arrive!

Without man having
a hand in it, they
came — no traps
or drovers, no nets
or anything else —

male and female,
Noah didn't even
need to sex them.

That wouldn't have been too
difficult with these creatures:
it needs no more than a glance
to see which is the he and which is the she:

but there are plenty of others which
are a lot more difficult to tell apart.

Clever fellow who can see the
difference between ♂ and ♀

Fortunately for Noah
and his family, all
they had to do was
to look on

and how they must have gasped at the continuous
performance going on!

Fleas and ticks probably came in greater numbers
than two by two...

Chances are that
among all these
animals there were
some the family
had never
seen before.

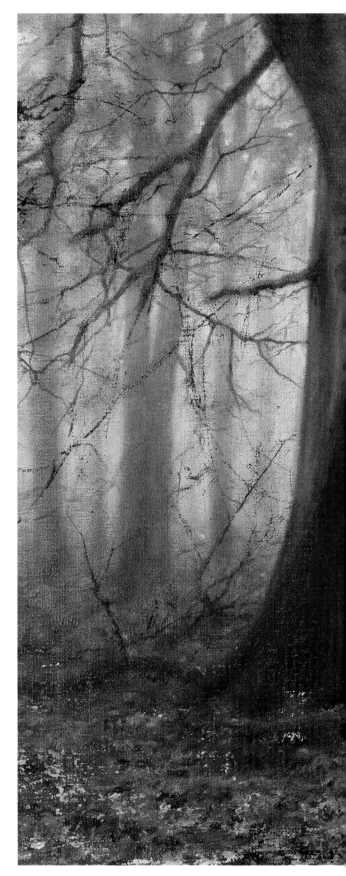

When you see a tapir coming
along for the first
time, you could well be
somewhat surprised...

... and the people who had laughed while the Ark was being built

they must have looked pretty surprised too! (but then they hadn't yet felt the brewing storm...)

Embarkation lasted seven days. Then Noah and all the chosen were inside

"and the Lord shut him in."

" ... the same day were all the fountains of the great deep broken up,
and the windows of heaven were opened,
And the rain was upon the earth forty days and forty nights, "

"And all flesh died that moved
upon the earth, both of fowl,
and of cattle, and of beast,
and of every creeping thing that
creepeth upon the earth,
and every man... "

"And the flood was forty days upon the earth;
and the waters increased, and bare up the Ark...

And the waters prevailed
exceedingly upon the earth;

and all the high hills, that
were under the whole
heaven, were covered."

Everything that carried the breath of life, everything on dry earth, died. (How frightful the stench must have been.)

You would think that fish, and especially the carnivorous aquatic animals, would be little troubled by the flood.

But who knows? Perhaps they were flung around so violently by the power of underwater explosions that everything perished...

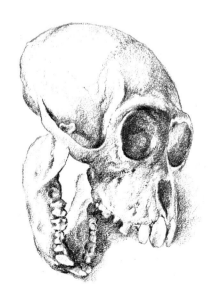

As a child I imagined it something like this:
Family Noah sitting snugly round the table, candlelight,
creaking timbers, animal noises now and then, and
outside the endlessly roaring heavy weather!

Strange that we don't see Noah's
Arks in toy shops here. The British
make all those beautiful animals—
an ark to go with them would make a handy
storage box at the same time.

When we used to go to Katwijk aan Zee for the summer holidays we had these beach toys.
Actually I have never been able to figure out exactly what to do with a sieve like this.

← I tried this a few times but never managed to catch so much as a shrimp with the thing.

But just think of having an ark with animals !!

and then playing with it in the warm pools on the beach (even more "real" in rainy weather).

But when I was little there were none of those beautifully reproduced toy animals.

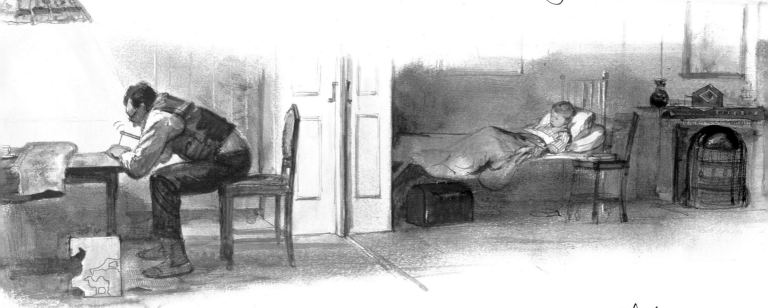

What I did have was a small zoo made by my good father.
From my bed, which was put in the back parlour
(I had been knocked down by a car),
I could keep an eye on things. Those were great evenings. I can hear the sound of the fret-saw still...

There were three cages, with wire-mesh. I had drawn the animals first on plywood.

Nowadays you can get some beautiful three-dimensional animals.
But it's a bit too late for me...
— I do have them now — a big tin full.
But now I am 51 and, apart from displaying them on a table now and then, I honestly do not know what to do with them ... maybe later the grandchildren will like them.

What it was like in the Ark (where they spent about a year)
the Bible does not tell us. One thing is certain: the animals
had to adjust considerably to the circumstances on board, they
couldn't just do what they wanted... certainly not this
↓

If it's all right with you, while I'm on the subject I'll put in some pictures of foxes here

I really love to paint, draw or model foxes!

A sight like this always makes
my heart beat a little faster!

This kind of carrying on was
certainly not wanted on board.

As for the fox, I had better leave it at that.

One way or another they must have quietened
down, perhaps into a sort of
hibernating state;
like that of the bear,
among others.

Also for the time being there simply wasn't the space for tussling and scrapping....

... nor was all that business of
reproduction wanted in
the Ark —

for that kind of thing you need quite a bit of room.

For the moment, such activities were out of the question.
The voyage was to last a good year
and it was of course important
for everyone to adjust as well
as possible.

After having spent
years in building,
Noah shouldn't
have had to act as
nanny, as well,

but...

what a terrific
opportunity for Noah
to observe all those
animals close up !

It could be that Noah had seen an aurochs before, but like this, face to face, is another matter altogether.

I imagine what fun Noah would have
had drawing his animals...
an opportunity like this never
comes again!

Models that have all the
time in the world,
what more could you want?

These are quick sketches
dashed off while working

and these somewhat more
fully worked out studies

and when there is time,
a serious formal
portrait

... when you are in the
same boat with them,
what a great pastime!

like Daniel, sitting in
the lions' den
among the big beasts
of prey

and not only an amusing pastime
while the bad weather rages outside,
but also a splendid opportunity
to get to know the animals better!

When drawing animals I often see a
likeness to people I know, I'd love to tell you
who these birds are like, but I'd better not.
(The one in the middle is <u>exactly</u> Mrs B......
when she comes into church wearing a new hat.)

← Mrs R......

Not only must Noah have made a lot of friends,
he also must have been lost in wonder looking
about him ; how had the
good Lord created it all !

There is just no escaping it, unless one is stone-blind.

*He must often have murmured words like those of Psalm 8 — that was very like him:*

O Lord our Lord, how excellent is thy name in all the earth!
    who hast set thy glory above the heavens.
Out of the mouth of babes and sucklings hast thou ordained
    strength because of thine enemies, that thou mightest
    still the enemy and the avenger.
When I consider thy heavens, the work of thy fingers, the
    moon and the stars, which thou hast ordained;
What is man, that thou art mindful of him? and the son of
    man, that thou visitest him?
For thou hast made him a little lower than the angels, and
    hast crowned him with glory and honour.
Thou madest him to have dominion over the works of thy
    hands; thou hast put all things under his feet:
All sheep and oxen, yea, and the beasts of the field;
The fowl of the air, and the fish of the sea, and whatsoever
    passeth through the paths of the seas.
O Lord our Lord, how excellent is thy name in all the earth!

The danger lies in the fact that we are over-familiar with things; when the egg hatches, a little chick comes out.

When one hamster climbs onto another, in the course of time we will have about six more — do we still find it amazing?

A cow is a cow, that is a fact — but we should at least be able to consider why a cow looks the way it does, and imagine how funny a cow would look if it had a tiger skin

or a set of antlers instead of horns

Why's the udder between the hind legs?

The elephant has it between the forelegs...

we know by now how a cow "should look", so we think this ← funny,

but let's be honest; if the cow had looked like this from the beginning we would just cycle by!

Anyway—the cow is like this.

an ordinary cow—
but just think
of inventing it...

at one time it was designed by the Creator of all things!

And that is something to marvel at,
like marvelling at every little butterfly
and meadow flower and the
tiniest water creatures.

How all those animals were invented out of nothing
is something I lie awake at night thinking about!!

   Just take the head for instance:
Our children used to have those plastic things
with which they could make
faces on a potato. If I am
not mistaken there were
several different noses.
Would the Almighty have
   set about it in the same way: a tray with all kinds of ears?

MOUSE

GAZELLE

DESERT FOX

POLECAT

BAT

WOLF

KOALA

HYENA

RHINOCEROS

TIGER

WILD BOAR

HARE

LYNX

AFRICAN ELEPHANT

all kinds of
different
ears...

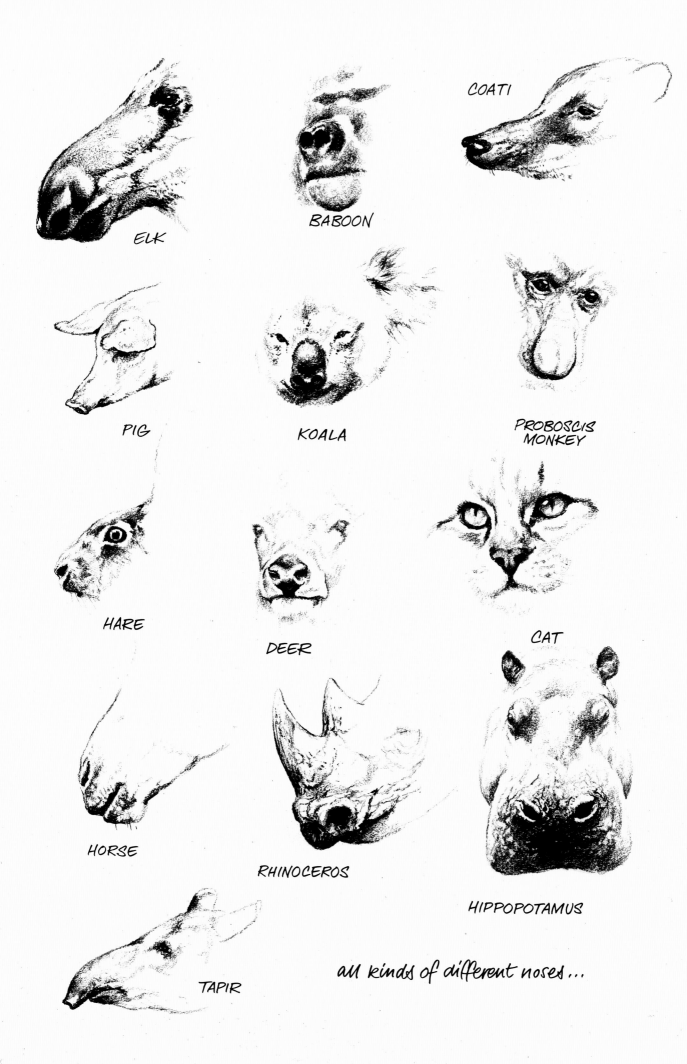

ELK

BABOON

COATI

PIG

KOALA

PROBOSCIS MONKEY

HARE

DEER

CAT

HORSE

RHINOCEROS

HIPPOPOTAMUS

TAPIR

*all kinds of different noses ...*

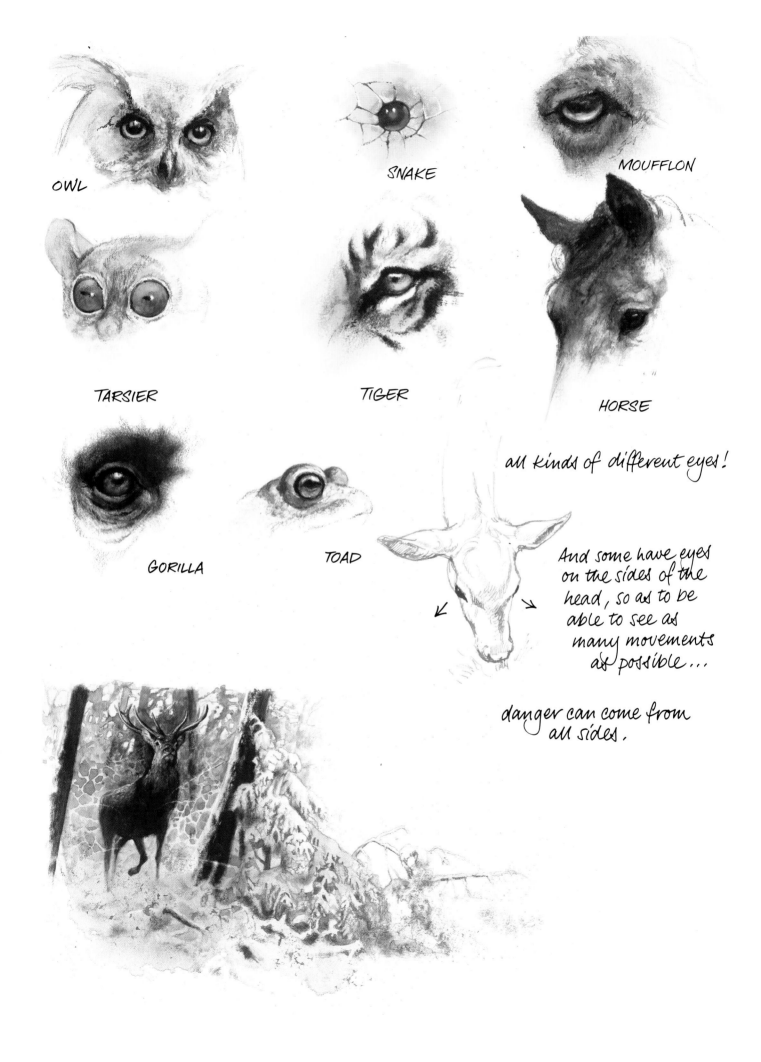

OWL

SNAKE

MOUFFLON

TARSIER

TIGER

HORSE

GORILLA

TOAD

all kinds of different eyes!

And some have eyes on the sides of the head, so as to be able to see as many movements as possible...

danger can come from all sides.

on the other hand,
the eyes of the hunters
are right in front...

...so they can estimate
distances accurately.

It is difficult
enough already for
a kestrel and a pine marten
to subsist from day to day.

All kinds of
different
beaks —

how could you
possibly think
them all up?

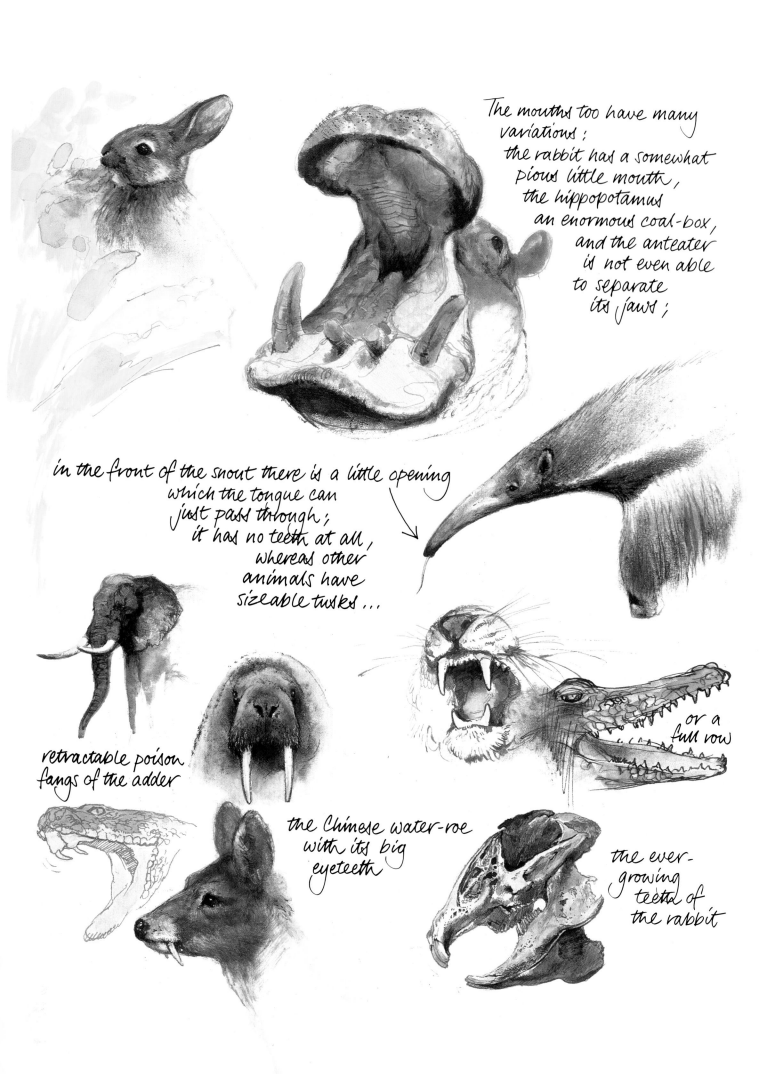

The mouths too have many variations:
the rabbit has a somewhat pious little mouth,
the hippopotamus an enormous coal-box,
and the anteater is not even able to separate its jaws;

in the front of the snout there is a little opening which the tongue can just pass through; it has no teeth at all, whereas other animals have sizeable tusks...

retractable poison fangs of the adder

the Chinese water-roe with its big eyeteeth

or a full row

the ever-growing teeth of the rabbit

Many animals have their big teeth in the upper jaw; the wild boar's are in the lower jaw.

The babiroussa of Celebes has teeth that grow from the upper jaw through the nose just in front of its eyes.

With all those variations
on the head theme
the Creator has still not
finished the job — the
things-on-the-head
come in for
their turn ...

with 4 horns!

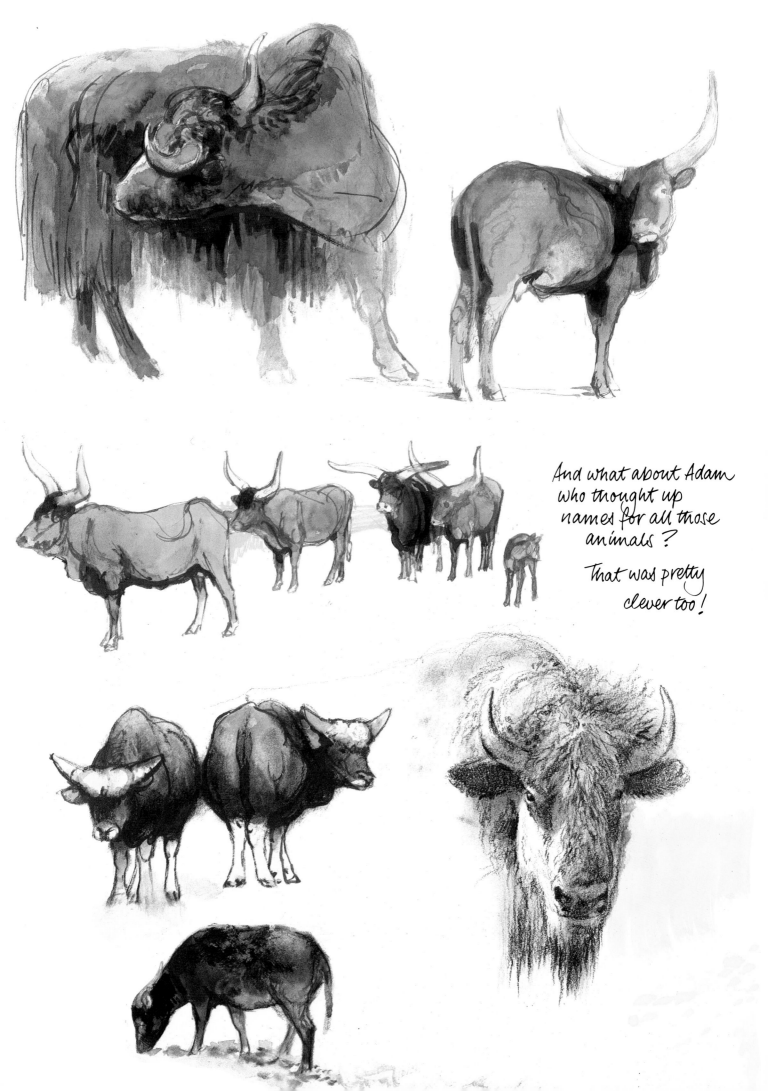

And what about Adam
who thought up
names for all those
animals?

That was pretty
clever too!

And then the box
containing the
ornaments is opened:
tufts, wattles,
moustaches, beards, in the boldest
forms and colours —there is
no end to it!

How do you come
up with something
like this?

Where he thought it necessary the Creator embellished his creatures with some painting; the badger got a pair of black strokes over his face that noticeably smartened him up,

and the racoon got his amusing crosswise mask

and others were given an apparently arbitrary stripe,

but how dull it would be without it!

A rich diversity in back-sides too — tails of all sorts and sizes !

Why does
the chicken
wear its tail
vertically

and the turkey horizontally?

And why has the lynx this kind
of stump and not a tail like
most cats,

and the roe-deer
no tail at all?

Every animal has its own foot: they must have noticed that:

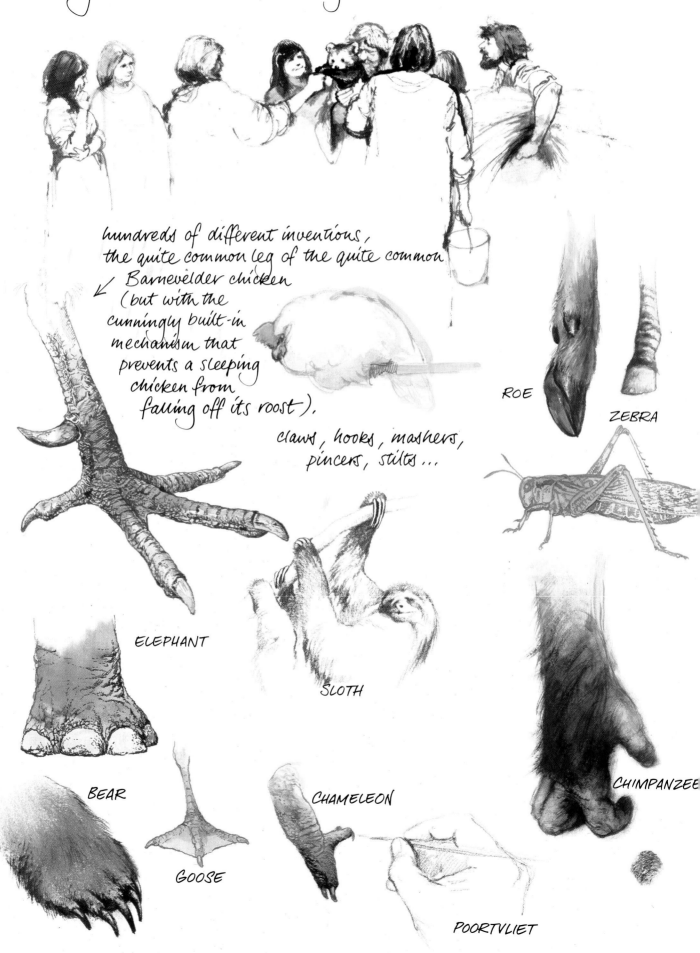

hundreds of different inventions,
the quite common leg of the quite common
Barnevelder chicken
(but with the
cunningly built-in
mechanism that
prevents a sleeping
chicken from
falling off its roost).

claws, hooks, mashers,
pincers, stilts...

ROE

ZEBRA

ELEPHANT

SLOTH

CHIMPANZEE

BEAR

GOOSE

CHAMELEON

POORTVLIET

One gets short legs
and the other
tall poles...

4, 6, 8, or more feet

and each one its own gait

everything is possible:
flying, creeping,
swimming, wriggling,
running, hovering,
sailing.

And then one by one they have to be given a new outfit.

The okapi gets a chic dress suit (very suitable for hot climates, too)

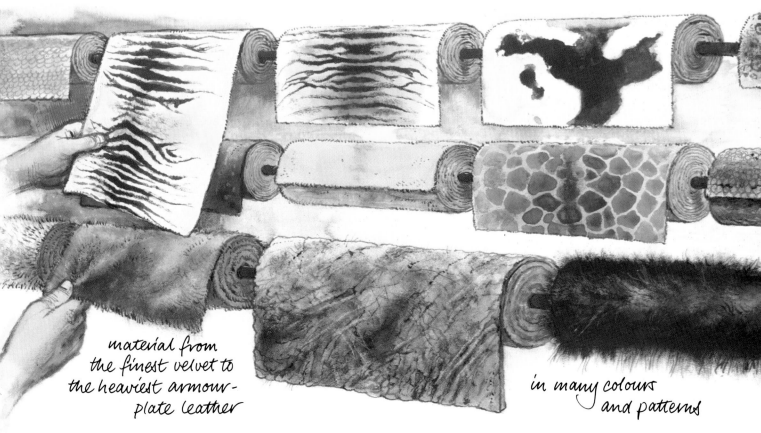

*material from
the finest velvet to
the heaviest armour-
plate leather*

*in many colours
and patterns*

camouflage outfits

an effective coat
for chilly weather

a rough, tough
coat for breaking
through undergrowth

*it has to be waterproof*

*it has to keep
out the cold*

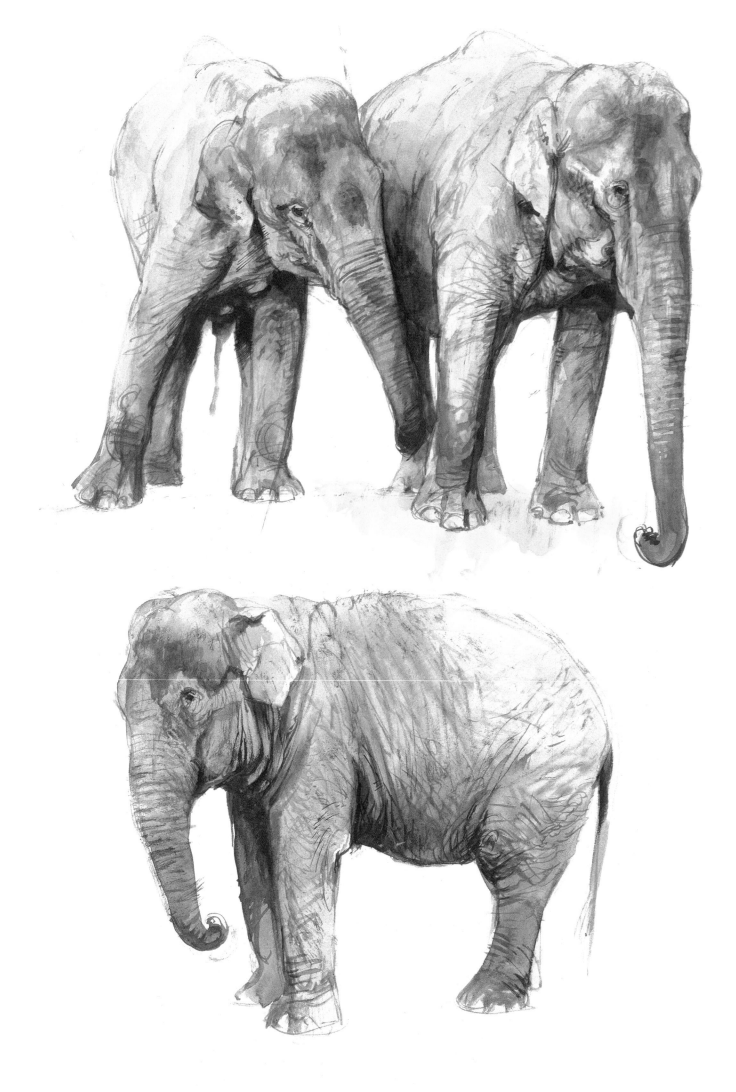

a thick leather suit
so that you are not
bothered by sharp
grasses or thorns

suits that can protect and also look good

In case Noah hadn't noticed it earlier — during all those
years of carpenting he hardly had eyes for anything else —
he must have seen it now:

how perfectly everything fits in !!

suits made of
feathers, hair, down,
scales, spines...

even to modelling
a parachute and
a carrying pouch →

there's no end to it !

We should marvel every time we
see an animal —
**how could the good Lord
ever have created all this!!**

But we do not marvel when we see an
'ordinary' bullfinch like this ←
or an 'ordinary' wood pigeon like this →

When do we say, "Hey, come and look
at this one"? When we see a horse
in wood pigeon colours?

or a cherry in a
panther design?

Protective
colouring is rather
nice, the Creator
must have thought,
but we mustn't overdo
things — therefore
rabbits aren't green;
they would have
become a plague!

and mice had so many
advantages already
with their speed, litheness,
protective colouring and
amazing ability to multiply
themselves, that at the last minute
they got a handicap; a sharp
urine odour so that they can be
tracked...

So here's another miracle to add to the list: every animal has its own smell! Unerringly the buck follows the scent of his own hind, no matter how frequently the scent has been crossed by other animals.

To make his presence known a buck stakes out his territory with his scent glands.

And so each has its own scent.
Nothing can be seen yet —
  but the wild boar knows very
well who, or what, is approaching.

And here's something else again.
Every animal makes its own sound.
When the woodcock calls,
the hen pheasant knows
it's not for her.

The roe-deer or
moufflon ewe don't
respond to the call of
the red deer.

Chirping, cheeping,
braying, bleating, croaking,
whistling, bellowing
and I don't know
what else...

horses,
titmice,
warblers,
gazelles
and
plovers...

we
hear them
speaking in
their own
language of
the great
deeds of
God!

Not only is there a difference between a hedgehog and a plaice, a panther and a crocodile — but animals of the same species differ among themselves, too.

The elephant that watches all those school-children filing past does actually notice that they all have different little faces ...

and we think that all those sheep look alike, as if they came out of a mould —

## What sheer arrogance !

as if we were the only ones — with a face of our own !

Well, you may be sure that animals have different faces just as much as we do

"The idea that this universe in all its million-fold order and precision is the result of blind chance is as credible as the idea that if a printshop blew up all the type would fall down again in the finished and faultless form of the dictionary."

Albert Einstein

Dreaming about Noah
and the Ark
I lingered mostly
in the stalls
of the mammals

I did not go into the
compartments of the
insects or reptiles.
I know that they too are
chock-full of wonders
but they were
beyond me...

We are advised to
go to the ants
to become wise,
but the fact is that
I would rather
paint the animals...

and fair's fair: with ants
you can't get this sort of
direct eye-to-eye contact.

No matter how wonderful the world of insects is,
I feel closer to animals that look at me
I understand them better...

With fellow creatures
that look you in the eye
in this way, you can
have a pleasant
exchange of thoughts

but that
less intelligent
look shows at once that
it is not so simple to
make contact with a
rather stupid turkey —————— and of course you can't have
a chat with this
one at all
that's for sure...

The bat can catch its prey with the help of radar — brilliant!
But I still prefer to see a polecat or sparrow hawk at work;
there's more to watch ...

"And God remembered Noah, and every living thing, and all the cattle that was with him in the ark: and God made a wind to pass over the earth, and the waters asswaged;...

And the ark rested in the seventh month, on the seventeenth day of the month, upon the mountains of Ararat...

At the end of forty days, Noah opened the window of the ark ... and he sent forth a raven, which went forth to and fro, until the waters were dried up from off the earth."

After that, at intervals he made three attempts to send out a dove; the first one returned with nothing achieved, the second one returned with a green olive leaf in its beak.

and the third dove Noah did not see again — and we don't read about a dove alighting until the baptism of Jesus in the Jordan (Matthew 3).

It must have
been a lively
scramble when
the animals ran
out onto the
promised land!

Altogether
it had taken
13 months before
Noah got his
animals onto dry
land again; a lot
must have been going on in his mind while he was watching them scatter...

"Every beast, every creeping thing,
and every fowl, and
whatsoever creepeth upon the earth,
after their kinds,
        went forth out of the Ark"

And God said to Noah and his sons:
"into your hand are they delivered."

And there they are, even if it's not necessarily
the best thing for them.
All things considered, they were very well off
with Noah in the ark.
But all the water of the sea won't wash away the fact
that things are gradually getting critical for many of them:
more frequently than ever, and without people
noticing, animal species vanish — for ever.

Well, we're not yet in a crisis situation.

Not yet ...

With some animals, we know that they will be here until the end of time.

In the last days the wolf and the lamb will dwell together (Isaiah);

The panther will lie down with the billy goat, the cattle and the bears will graze together, and the lion will eat straw like the cattle...

We'll have to get used to that!

I do wonder what the lion
fed on when he felt firm
ground under his feet—
of course he couldn't
immediately catch one
of the two zebras...!

Whatever happened to the Ark, and afterwards —
the fact is that we are all in this together,
and that's what matters.

I'm so glad that the animals were included !!!
I could not imagine life without animals —

*without "wildlife"*

Mijnheer
Pastoor

Max

Tim

nor without our "domesticated" companions (shown here on the doors of my TV cabinet).

How did the good Lord come up with all this !!!!

Animals are constantly
offering something
new to watch.

My greatest joy is painting
them day in and
day out !

So hurrah
for Noah!

Noah took us all with him across the waters.
For this surely he deserves a statue — but oddly
enough, I have never heard of one.
As far as I know, not even a tiny street
has been named after him.

Gratefully reaping the benefits, I am happy to paint a hare — sometimes as a portrait, at other times against his background, so we can get some idea of how he lives.

One way or another I think
that the poem below
should have a place
in this book.

Anna Sauper, a six-year-old
girl from Austria,
wrote it when a little
orphaned hare she
had tried to raise
by bottle-feeding did
not pull through in
the end.

OH MY DARLING PET
i HAVE LOVED YOU
AND LOVE YOU
STILL.
+ IN THE NAME OF
THE FATHER
AND THE SON
AND THE HOLY SPIRIT.
        AMEN.

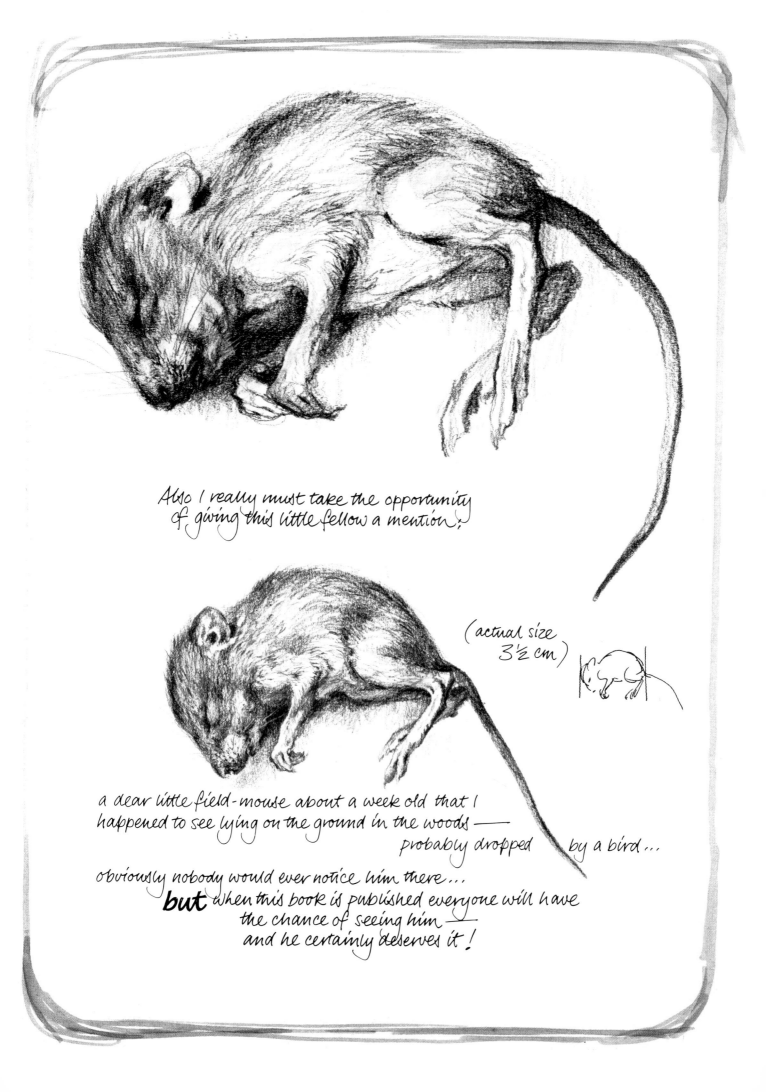

Also I really must take the opportunity of giving this little fellow a mention:

(actual size 3½ cm)

a dear little field-mouse about a week old that I happened to see lying on the ground in the woods — probably dropped by a bird...

obviously nobody would ever notice him there...
**but** when this book is published everyone will have the chance of seeing him — and he certainly deserves it!

Those who have not been brought up with the idea
really should make an effort to become more
interested — the Creator hasn't made all this for
no reason at all.

Just a little joke;
how many people would notice something
odd about this animal?

The body is that
of a roe deer and
the head is a
kangaroo's.

Come to think of it, when they reached dry land
it must have been very important for the nervously scurrying
little animals not to lose sight of one another

two or three jumps for joy in different
directions and they would have lost one
another for ever!

the larger animals may
not have had to worry

but others were so
intent on security
that they got
going at once...

Noah must always
have had a soft spot for
new young animals.

Everyone likes seeing young
animals, but for Noah it was as if
he had become a father again himself.

It must have been
heart-warming — the
continual renewal of life.

After the flood Noah and his family must have seen water with different eyes ... with every downpour they were reminded again !

Perhaps it's a good thing when something happens which makes us see everything with different eyes (though preferably without the occurrence of a natural disaster);

then for once we stare open-mouthed!

then it's not
JUST ANOTHER COW
but
A COW! JUST LOOK!

The other day I saw a cow and a magpie facing each other. I was just thinking: "That is a thing you don't often see, two black-and-white creatures together ..." and then a black-and-white cat came along.

 ha!

An ordinary pheasant, an ordinary
sleeping dog — what a pity they do not
astonish us ... they are so
marvellously fashioned.

So — go to the zoo
and marvel.

I heard on the news
that there are only about 1000 okapis left, only a few
bantengs and around 1000 small pandas—
in the whole world!  I didn't know that before.

With the water up to our necks,
so to speak, it is high
time to build
another ark.

When you look
around in the
countryside you do see
many such "arks":
but always with that
gigantic "eggcup"
next to it—

and those arks are already
chock-full of chickens
or pigs...

Will we ever build
a proper ark for the
little panda?

Having got to this point, I have two ways of
seeing things—
I can sigh that the boat is wrecked and
lament our lost opportunities, our foolish
management, the extinct species, the
deforestation, the dumping of toxic waste
and so on ...
but that was not the purpose of it all.

Right from the beginning I was aiming to produce a rather
    different response — a heartfelt hymn of praise.
        Honour to whom honour is due!

    Why should I try to find other words for it than
            those of Psalm 104 ?

# Psalm 104

*The Lord's glory in creation*

Bless the Lord, O my soul. O Lord my God, thou art very
great; thou art clothed with honour and majesty.
Who coverest thyself with light as with a garment: who
stretchest out the heavens like a curtain:
Who layeth the beams of his chambers in the waters: who
maketh the clouds his chariot: who walketh upon the
wings of the wind:
Who maketh his angels spirits; his ministers a flaming fire:

Who laid the foundations of the earth, that it should not be
removed for ever.
Thou coveredst it with the deep as with a garment: the
waters stood above the mountains.
At thy rebuke they fled; at the voice of thy thunder they
hasted away.
They go up by the mountains; they go down by the valleys
unto the place which thou hast founded for them.
Thou hast set a bound that they may not pass over; that
they turn not again to cover the earth.

He sendeth the springs into the valleys, which run among
the hills.
They give drink to every beast of the field: the wild asses
quench their thirst.
By them shall the fowls of the heaven have their habitation,
which sing among the branches.
He watereth the hills from his chambers: the earth is
satisfied with the fruit of thy works.

He causeth the grass to grow for the cattle, and herb for the
service of man: that he may bring forth food out of the
earth:
And wine that maketh glad the heart of man, and oil to
make his face to shine, and bread which strengtheneth
man's heart.
The trees of the Lord are full of sap; the cedars of Lebanon,
which he hath planted;
Where the birds make their nests: as for the stork, the fir
trees are her house.

The high hills are a refuge for the wild goats; and the rocks
for the conies.
He appointed the moon for seasons: the sun knoweth his
going down.
Thou makest darkness, and it is night: wherein all the beasts
of the forest do creep forth.
The young lions roar after their prey, and seek their meat
from God.
The sun ariseth, they gather themselves together, and lay
them down in their dens.
Man goeth forth unto his work and to his labour until the
evening.

O Lord, how manifold are thy works! in wisdom hast thou
made them all: the earth is full of thy riches.
So is this great and wide sea, wherein are things creeping
innumerable, both small and great beasts.
There go the ships: there is that leviathan, whom thou hast
made to play therein.
These wait all upon thee; that thou mayest give them their
meat in due season.
That thou givest them they gather: thou openest thine
hand, they are filled with good.
Thou hidest thy face, they are troubled: thou takest away
their breath, they die, and return to their dust.
Thou sendest forth thy spirit, they are created: and thou
renewest the face of the earth.

The glory of the Lord shall endure for ever: the Lord shall
rejoice in his works.
He looketh on the earth, and it trembleth: he toucheth the
hills, and they smoke.
I will sing unto the Lord as long as I live: I will sing praise to
my God while I have my being.
My meditation of him shall be sweet: I will be glad in the
Lord.
Let the sinners be consumed out of the earth, and let the
wicked be no more. Bless thou the Lord, O my soul.
Praise ye the Lord.

*It is to be hoped too that our
children's children may
also continue to be glad...*

So, to those who care :

the people of the World Wildlife Fund
are engaged in many ark-like projects
in various places.
They deserve a helping hand,

This book will be welcomed with enthusiasm
by all lovers of nature, young and old.

For almost twenty-five years now I have
been fighting to preserve flora and fauna,
so that human life does not become impoveri-
shed or unbearable. I do believe this really
beautiful book will stimulate the desire
of its readers to help those of us who are
working for the preservation of our natural
environment and all that is involved in
it.

Prince of the Netherlands